Jazz says "Goodbye"

A book for anyone who has lost someone

Words and photos: Victoria Bryan
In memory of Jean Bryan

Proceeds will benefit
The Martlets Hospice, Hove

Jazz lived with her mum for 14 years. They enjoyed doing things together, especially going for walks along the seafront and on the lawns, where they often talked to friends.

One day, Jazz's mum wasn't there anymore and Jazz was told that she had died. Someone else started looking after her and Jazz felt very alone and confused, even with other people around.

Jazz didn't know what to make of it and she missed her mum a lot. She felt very sad and sometimes she was angry. She wanted to be by herself.

She saw other dogs who looked happy
because they were at home or at work
with their families.

Jazz thought it wasn't fair.

Jazz tried going to the places
where she used to go with her mum
but it wasn't the same by herself.

She spent a lot of time sitting alone because she didn't really want to talk to anyone.

She found herself eating too
much, as she tried to fill up
the emptiness inside.

Sometimes Jazz painted, or took photos, or wrote stories. When she did that, it helped her understand her feelings.

When Jazz started going out again, she noticed that
she felt happier after walking or playing with her ball.

One day, she saw Snowy and after chatting with him and his person, she realized how much she missed her friends.

As soon as she got home, she gave away her television because watching a screen for hours by herself made her feel blue.

She started looking for friends when she went out. It took time but little by little, she began enjoying being with others again.

It felt good to see Peggy Sue and Echo, Boris sitting on a bench, and Max waiting for his person.

Jazz talked to her friend Gracie and Gracie's mum about what had happened. She found that talking helped her feel better.

She made new friends, like Boo, and she told him about her mum and their walks.

It was fun for Jazz to see that her friends Millie and Daphne and Echo had learned new things.

Jazz liked playing with friends,
like Ella, who had known her mum.

Jazz didn't forget her mum.

Jazz knew her mum would be happy that she
was enjoying new places. In fact, sometimes she felt
like her mum was with her, wherever she went.

Jazz found that she liked going back to the places where she and her mum used to go. She remembered having fun with her mum and those memories were comforting to her.

Jazz was ready for more fun in the future.

Contents

I like walking to school with Grandad.

He went to the same school as me ...

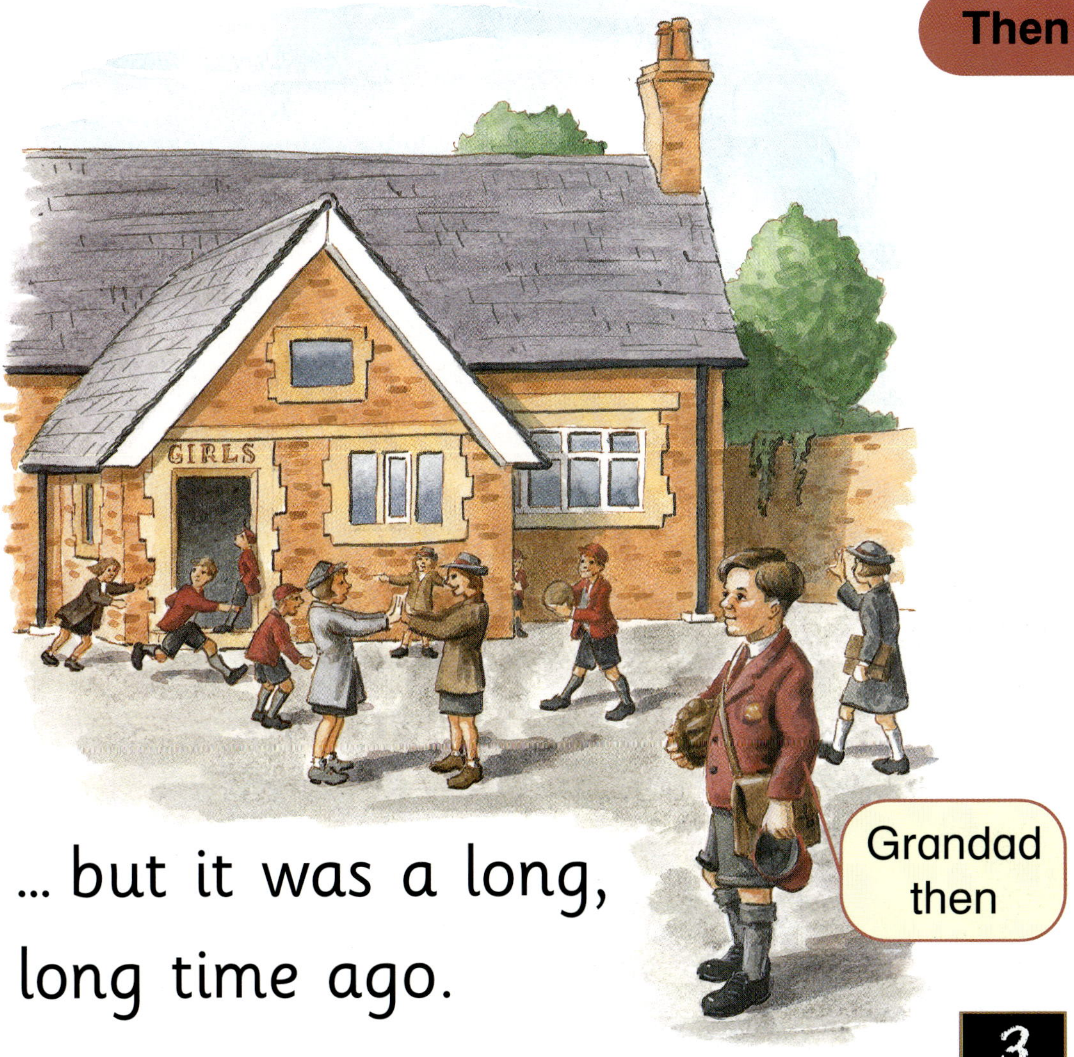

... but it was a long, long time ago.

The boys had to go in one door.

Boys wore caps

The girls had to go
in the other door.

Grandad's teacher was strict.

If Grandad talked in class ...

Grandad's desk

... he had to stand in the corner.

If he did it again ...

... he had to hold out his hand.

At playtime Grandad had some milk.

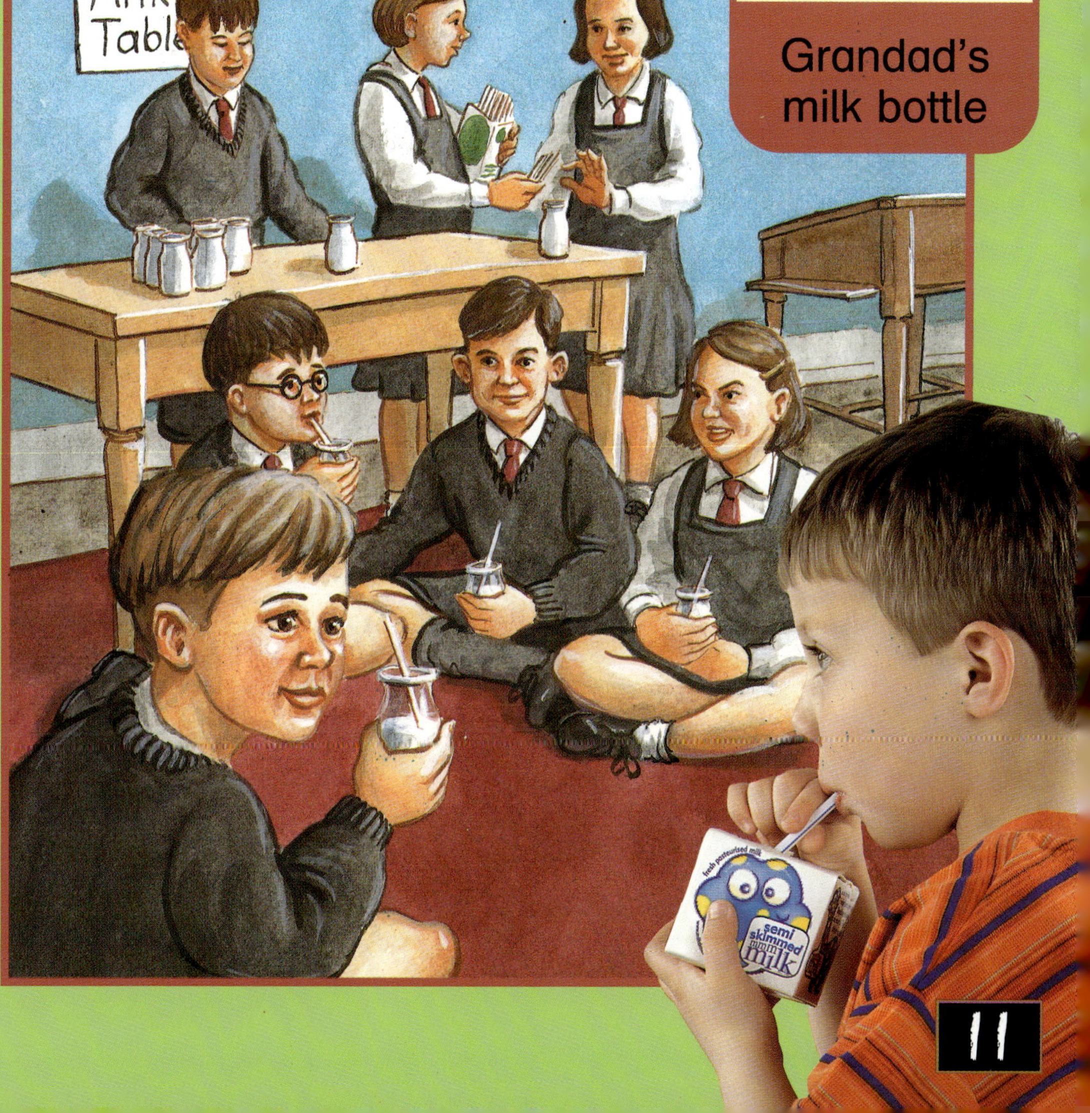

Grandad's milk bottle

Then he played football with his friends.

Grandad's football

Grandad's best lesson was painting.

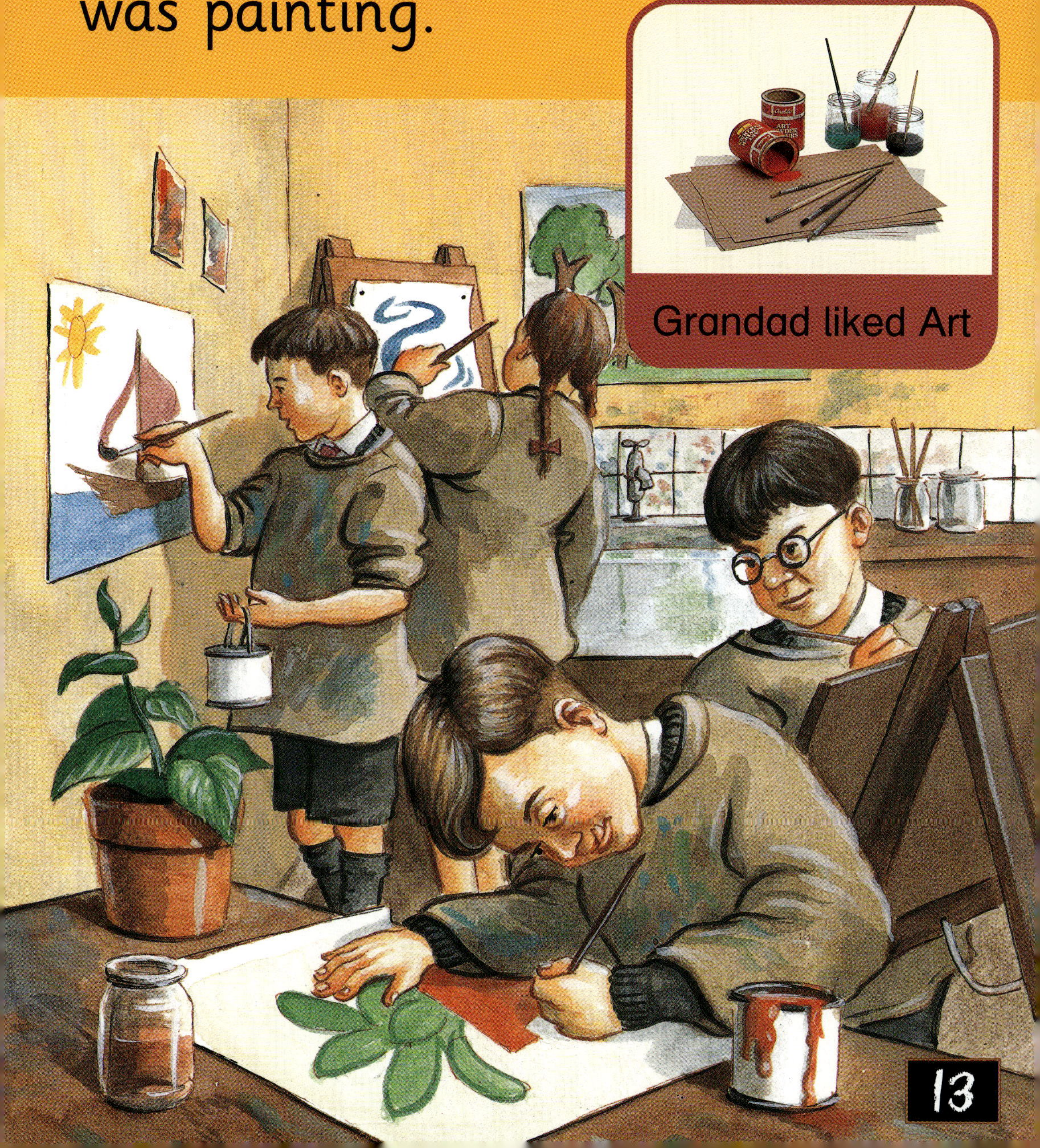

Grandad liked Art

His best school dinner
was meat pie.

After school, Grandad liked walking home on his own.

But I like walking home
with Grandad.